To Gran
love from
John.
Christmas '95'

# REFLECTIONS

## On Prayer

# REFLECTIONS ON PRAYER

Text Copyright © 1993 Warren W. Wiersbe
Extracted from WITH THE WORD, published in the USA by Thomas Nelsc
Inc., Nashville, Tn.

Photographs copyright © Noël Halsey

Published by Nelson Word Ltd 1993.

ISBN 0-85009-225-6    (Australia ISBN 1-86258-141-X)

All Scripture quotations are from The New Century Version, copyright © 198'
1988, 1993 by Word Publishing.  Used by permission.

Reproduced, printed and bound in Great Britain for Nelson Word Ltd., by Is
Press, Didcot, Oxon., England.

Photographs used in this book were taken at the following locations:

| Front Cover | Grand Union Canal, Milton Keynes |
| Page 8/9 | Israel |
| Page 10/11 | Sea of Galilee, Israel |
| Page 12/13 | Devon |
| Page 14/15 | Fiji |
| Page 16/17 | Cape Town, South Africa |
| Page 18/19 | Ilfracombe, Devon |
| Page 20/21 | Bancroft, Milton Keynes |
| Page 22/23 | Bay of Islands, New Zealand |
| Page 24/25 | Bay of Islands, New Zealand |
| Page 26/27 | Bay of Islands, New Zealand |
| Page 28/29 | Hyde Park, London |

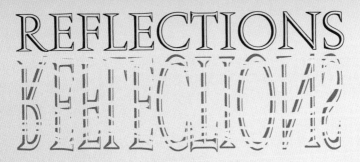

# REFLECTIONS

## *On Prayer*

**WORD PUBLISHING**
Nelson Word Ltd
Milton Keynes, England

WORD AUSTRALIA
Kilsyth, Australia

WORD COMMUNICATIONS LTD
Vancouver, B.C., Canada

STRUIK CHRISTIAN BOOKS (PTY LTD)
Cape Town, South Africa

JOINT DISTRIBUTORS SINGAPORE —
ALBY COMMERCIAL ENTERPRISES PTE LTD
and
CAMPUS CRUSADE

CHRISTIAN MARKETING NEW ZEALAND LTD
Havelock North, New Zealand

JENSCO LTD
Hong Kong

SALVATION BOOK CENTRE
Malaysia

WARREN W. WIERSBE

WORD
BOOKS

# PSALM 102
## *(verses 1–16)*

LORD, listen to my prayer;
  let my cry for help come to you.
Do not hide from me
  in my time of trouble.
Pay attention to me.
  When I cry for help, answer me quickly.

My life is passing away like smoke,
  and my bones are burned up with fire.
My heart is like grass
  that has been cut and dried.
  I forget to eat.
Because of my grief,
  my skin hangs on my bones.
I am like a desert owl,
  like an owl living among the ruins.
I lie awake.
  I am like a lonely bird on a housetop.
All day long enemies insult me;
  those who make fun of me use my name as
    a curse.
I eat ashes for food,
  and my tears fall into my drink.
Because of your great anger,
  you have picked me up and thrown me
    away.
My days are like a passing shadow;
  I am like dried grass.

But, LORD, you rule for ever,
  and your fame goes on and on.
You will come and have mercy on
      Jerusalem,
  because the time has now come to be kind
      to her;
  the right time has come.
Your servants love even her stones;
  they even care about her dust.
Nations will fear the name of the LORD,
  and all the kings on earth will honour you.
The LORD will rebuild Jerusalem;
  there his glory will be seen.

God enjoys endless years, but we endure shortened days (vv. 23–24), troubled days (v. 2), days that disappear like smoke, grass, and a shadow (vv. 3, 4, 11). We sit alone like birds in a desert and dying patients in a hospital (vv. 5–9). How depressing!

Do you ever have days like that? If you do, beware. Looking at yourself and your feelings will only make things worse. Do what the writer of this penitential psalm did: look by faith to the Lord. Things will be different when you look from yourself to God and say, "But You."

*"But You shall endure"* (12–22). If you know Jesus Christ by faith, you possess eternal life (1 John 5:11–13). So, living in a world of death and decay need not be a threat to you because you will live for ever with the Lord (1 Thess. 4:13–18).

*"But You are the same"* (25–28). As you grow older, you may find yourself resisting change. Loved ones move away or die, your body weakens, the world changes, and it is easy to become bitter and afraid. But God does not change (Heb. 13:5–8), and He is your Friend and Guide to the very end (Ps. 73:24).

The temporary things will change, but the things eternal will last (2 Cor. 4:11–18).

## *"Abide with Me"*

*Swift to its close ebbs out life's little day;*
*Earth's joys grow dim, its glories pass away;*
*Change and decay in all around I see;*
*O Thou who changest not, abide with me.*

*Henry Francis Lyte*

# PSALM 70

God, come quickly and save me.
   LORD, hurry to help me.
Let those who are trying to kill me
   be ashamed and disgraced.
Let those who want to hurt me
   run away in disgrace.
Let those who make fun of me
   stop because of their shame.
But let all those who worship you
   rejoice and be glad.
Let those who love your salvation
   always say, "Praise the greatness of God."

I am poor and helpless;
   God, hurry to me.
You help me and save me.
   LORD, do not wait.

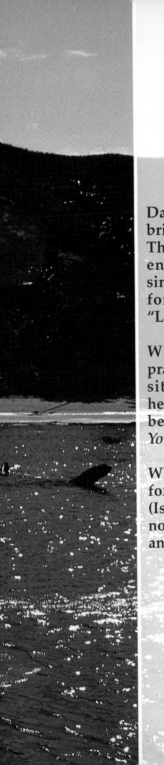

David was in a hurry when he wrote this brief psalm because God was *not* in a hurry! Three times he cried, "Make haste!" and he ended with, "Do not delay!" Like Peter sinking into the water, he did not have time for a long prayer. All he could cry was, "Lord, save me!" (See Matt. 14:30.)

Why does God delay answering your prayers? Surely He can see your desperate situation. He promises to give "grace to help in time of need" (Heb. 4:16), which can be translated "grace for well-timed help". *Your Father's timing is never wrong.*

When God waits, He may have a better gift for you than what you are asking Him for (Isa. 30:18). His delays are neither denials nor defeats, so put your times in His hands and wait on the Lord (Ps. 31:15).

# PSALM 61

God, hear my cry;
   listen to my prayer.

I call to you from the ends of the earth
   when I am afraid.
   Carry me away to a high mountain.
You have been my protection,
   like a strong tower against my enemies.

Let me live in your Holy Tent for ever.
   Let me find safety in the shelter of your
     wings.
God, you have heard my promises.
   You have given me what belongs to
     those who fear you.
Give the king a long life;
   let him live many years.
Let him rule in the presence of God for ever.
   Protect him with your love and truth.

Then I will praise your name for ever,
   and every day I will keep my promises.

*Distance.* No matter how far away you go, God hears your prayers, for His ears are open to the cries of His children (Ps. 34:15). David was far from the house of God, yet the Lord heard his prayer and answered.

*Depth.* No matter how far down you sink, God can lift you up. When life overwhelms you, take time to pray. Let God lift you up and put you on the Rock that will never sink.

*Danger.* Prayer brings you into the Holy of Holies, under the shadow of His wings (Exod. 25:20), where God's glory dwells. God preserves and protects His own until that hour when He calls them to Himself.

*Delight.* Do you find delight in prayer, or is prayer only an "emergency exercise" to get you out of trouble? David ended the psalm with an expression of praise and an affirmation of obedience. Prayer changes things, but prayer also changes people, starting with the one who does the praying!

# PSALM 6

Lord, don't punish me when you are
    angry;
  don't punish me when you are very angry.
Lord, have mercy on me because I am weak.
  Heal me, Lord, because my bones ache.
I am very upset.
  Lord, how long will it be?

Lord, return and save me;
  save me because of your love.
Dead people don't remember you;
  those in the grave don't praise you.

I am tired of crying to you.
  Every night my bed is wet with tears;
  my bed is soaked from my crying.
My eyes are weak from so much crying;
  they are weak from crying about my
    enemies.

Get away from me, all you who do evil,
  because the Lord has heard my crying.
The Lord has heard my cry for help;
  the Lord will answer my prayer.
All my enemies will be ashamed and
    troubled.
  They will turn and suddenly leave in
    shame.

This psalm grew out of an experience of sickness and pain, when David thought he was going to die. Besides that, he had to put up with the attacks of his enemies who *wanted* him to die. It was a time of deep discouragement for David, but he did not waver in his faith.

As he prayed, he asked for mercy for his body (vv. 1–2) and his soul (vv. 3–5). Mercy means that God does not give us what we deserve, and grace means that He gives us what we do not deserve. What a loving God He is!

David reminded God of his tears of repentance and confession (vv. 6–7). His bed should have been a place of rest, but it had become a place of trial as God chastened him.

But there is a happy ending: David was assured and his enemies were ashamed (vv. 8–10)! God heard and answered his prayers! When the night is dark and long, keep on trusting, and the dawn will come in God's good time.

# PSALM 105

*(verses 1–9)*

Give thanks to the LORD and pray to him.
  Tell the nations what he has done.
Sing to him; sing praises to him.
  Tell about all his miracles.
Be glad that you are his;
  let those who seek the LORD be happy.
Depend on the LORD and his strength;
  always go to him for help.

Remember the miracles he has done;
  remember his wonders and his decisions.
You are descendants of his servant Abraham,
  the children of Jacob, his chosen people.
He is the LORD our God.
  His laws are for all the world.

He will keep his agreement for ever;
  he will keep his promises always.
He will keep the agreement he made with
      Abraham
  and the promise he made to Isaac.

The previous psalm extols the Creator, while this one exalts the Redeemer and His providential care for His people, Israel.

*His deeds* (1–6). When you read the history of Israel, you are encouraged by God's mighty and marvellous deeds wrought for His needy people (Rom. 15:4). You want to praise Him, rejoice in Him, seek Him, and tell others about Him.

*His covenant* (7–15). God bound Himself by an oath to only one nation, Israel. He gave His promise to Abraham (Gen. 12:1–3) and then reaffirmed it to his descendants. The covenant was their assurance that they would inherit the land. God's new covenant people have the assurance that their future inheritance is secure (Matt. 26:26–29); Heb. 8:6–13).

*His servants* (16–45). God sent Joseph to Egypt to preserve Jacob's family so they could become a nation. He sent Moses to Egypt to deliver His people. He sent Aaron to assist Moses and serve as high priest for a sinful people. God always has a man or woman ready to send when a job must be done. He waits to hear you say, "Here am I! Send me!" (Isa. 6:8).

# PSALM 4

Answer me when I pray to you,
  my God who does what is right.
Make things easier for me when I am in trouble.
Have mercy on me and hear my prayer.

People, how long will you turn my honour
    into shame?
How long will you love what is false and
    look for new lies?
You know that the LORD has chosen for
    himself those who are loyal to him.
  The LORD listens when I pray to him.

When you are angry, do not sin.
  Think about these things quietly
  as you go to bed.

Do what is right as a sacrifice to the LORD
  and trust the LORD.

Many people ask,
  "Who will give us anything good?"
  LORD, be kind to us.
But you have made me very happy,
  happier than they are,
    even with all their grain and new wine.
I go to bed and sleep in peace,
  because, LORD, only you keep me safe.

David wrote this psalm as he was about to retire for the night (v. 8). He could not do much about the war around him, but he could do something about the war within him. He did not want to lie in bed and worry, so he committed himself and his situation to the Lord.

*He asked* (1–3). Asking the Lord for help is still a good way to deal with inner turmoil (Phil. 4:6–7).

*He believed* (4–5). He faced his anger honestly and gave it to the Lord (Eph. 4:26). Instead of lying in bed and thinking about your problems, meditate on the Lord and offer Him sacrifices of praise.

*He received* (6–8). In the darkness, he saw the face of God and received light. In his sorrow, he discovered the gift of gladness. In the time of battle, he received peace. God did not immediately change the situation, but He did change David; He can do the same for you.

# PSALM 140

LORD, rescue me from evil people;
  protect me from cruel people
who make evil plans,
  who always start fights.
They make their tongues sharp as a snake's;
  their words are like snake poison.

LORD, guard me from the power of wicked
      people;
  protect me from cruel people
who plan to trip me up.
The proud hid a trap for me.
  They spread out a net beside the road;
  they set traps for me.

I said to the LORD, "You are my God."
  LORD, listen to my prayer for help.
LORD God, my mighty Saviour,
  you protect me in battle.
LORD, do not give the wicked what they
      want.
  Don't let their plans succeed,
  or they will become proud.

Those around me have planned trouble.
  Now let it come to them.
Let burning coals fall on them.
  Throw them into the fire
  or into pits from which they cannot escape.
Don't let liars settle in the land.
  Let evil quickly hunt down cruel people.

I know the LORD will get justice for the poor
  and will defend the needy in court.
Good people will praise his name;
  honest people will live in his presence.

Satan fights anyone who is doing the will of God, and David was no exception. You must pray for Christian leaders especially, for they are prime targets for the evil one. The enemy has two favourite weapons: poisonous tongues (vv. 1–3) and hidden traps (vv. 4–5). He slanders God's leaders (sometimes using the lips of professed Christians), and he sets traps for them, hoping to trip them up.

David depended on prayer (vv. 6–11), God's promise (v. 12), and praise (v. 13). God hates a lying tongue (Prov. 6:17) and will one day judge slanderers. Meanwhile, maintain your character before God and let Him take care of your reputation. So live that when people hear lies about you, they will not believe them.

# PSALM 56 (verses 1–11)

God, be merciful to me because
    people are chasing me;
  the battle has pressed me all day long.
My enemies have chased me all day;
  there are many proud people fighting me.

When I am afraid, I will trust you.
I praise God for his word.
  I trust God, so I am not afraid.
  What can human beings do to me?

All day long they twist my words;
  all their evil plans are against me.
They wait.  They hide.
  They watch my steps,
  hoping to kill me.

God, do not let them escape;
  punish the foreign nations in your anger.
You have recorded my troubles.
  You have kept a list of my tears.
  Aren't they in your records?

On the day I call for help, my enemies will
    be defeated.
  I know that God is on my side.
I praise God for his word to me;
  I praise the LORD for his word.
I trust in God.  I will not be afraid.
  What can people do to me?

David prayed this prayer while he was in danger in enemy country (1 Sam. 21:10–15). After God delivered him, he wrote Psalm 34 as an expression of praise. When you are in the midst of trouble, remember these truths about God.

*God sees where you are* (8a). David should not have been in Gath to begin with, but the Lord was gracious to go with him and help him. God understands your situation far better than you do!

*God knows how you feel* (8b). He not only knows your tears, but He records them and retains them! Why? So that one day He may transform them into gems of joy and glory. No tears are ever wasted when you follow Him.

*God hears when you call* (9). Terrors and tears must be handled with trust (vv. 3–4, 10–11). But be sure your motive is not just deliverance. He delivers us that we might delight in Him and serve Him (vv. 12–13). The highest purpose of prayer is the glory of God.

# PSALM 54

God, save me because of who you are.
  By your strength show that I am
    innocent.
Hear my prayer, God;
  listen to what I say.

Strangers turn against me,
  and cruel men want to kill me.
  They do not care about God.

See, God will help me;
  the Lord will support me.

Let my enemies be punished with their
    own evil.
  Destroy them because you are loyal to me.

I will offer a sacrifice as a special gift to you.
  I will thank you, LORD, because you are
    good.
You have saved me from all my troubles,
  and I have seen my enemies defeated.

David had not bothered the Ziphites, yet they turned against him to win favour with King Saul (1 Sam. 23:15–23). The world does not love God's people and even strangers will create problems for you while you seek to serve the Lord.

Do what David did: pray for God to take charge, protect you and vindicate you against your enemies. God hears (v. 2) and God helps (v. 4). When the answer comes, be sure you take time to praise the Lord (v. 6).

# PSALM 28

LORD, my Rock, I call out to you for help.
  Do not be deaf to me.
If you are silent,
  I will be like those in the grave.
Hear the sound of my prayer,
  when I cry out to you for help.
I raise my hands
  towards your Most Holy Place.

Don't drag me away with the wicked,
  with those who do evil.
They say "Peace" to their neighbours,
  but evil is in their hearts.
Pay them back for what they have done,
  for their evil deeds.
Pay them back for what they have done;
  give them their reward.
They don't understand what the LORD has
      done
  or what he has made.
So he will knock them down
  and not lift them up.

Praise the LORD,
  because he heard my prayer for help.
The Lord is my strength and shield.
  I trust him, and he helps me.
I am very happy,
  and I praise him with my song.

The LORD is powerful;
  he gives victory to his chosen one.
Save your people
  and bless those who are your own.
  Be their shepherd and carry them for ever.

*Requesting* (1–5). David's enemies were undermining his reputation and his work, so he turned to the Lord with two special requests: that God would speak to him (vv. 1–2) and that God would save him (vv. 3–5). God speaks to us in answered prayer. "If You are silent," said David, "I might just as well be dead! And if You don't deliver me, You are treating me like the enemy!" Pretty powerful arguments!

*Rejoicing* (6–9). God heard him and helped him, and He does the same for you today as you trust Him. You can rejoice in the Lord even when you cannot rejoice in yourselves or your circumstances. Trust God to be your strength, your song, and your salvation (Isa. 12:2). He is the faithful Shepherd who can carry both you and your burdens.

# PSALM 99
*(verses 1–7)*

The LORD is king.
  Let the peoples shake with fear.
He sits between the gold creatures with wings.
  Let the earth shake.
The LORD in Jerusalem is great;
  he is supreme over all the peoples.
Let them praise your name;
  it is great, holy and to be feared.

The King is powerful and loves justice.
  LORD, you made things fair;
you have done what is fair and right
  for the people of Jacob.
Praise the LORD our God,
  and worship at the Temple, his footstool.
  He is holy.

Moses and Aaron were among his priests,
  and Samuel was among his worshippers.
They called to the LORD,
  and he answered them.
He spoke to them from the pillar of cloud.
  They kept the rules and laws he gave them.

"He is holy" (vv. 3, 5, 9), and He is high (v. 2); therefore, give God the honour due Him.

*Fear Him* (1–3). The greatness of God makes the earth shake, and it should make the people tremble (Isa. 64:1–5). Even the demons tremble when they think of God (James 2:19). It is frightening to hear how carelessly many people speak *about* God or *to* God. It is even more frightening to see how carelessly people live, as though God will never require an accounting from them.

*Exalt Him* (4–5). The Lord is exalted in strength, righteousness, and holiness. One way to exalt Him is by your worship, but you must back that up by a consistent walk. Christ should be magnified in your body so that the lost around you may realise how great He is (1 Cor. 6:19–20; Phil. 1:19–26).

*Call on Him* (6–9). Three great men of prayer are mentioned to encourage you in your praying. They were not perfect, but they heard God's word, obeyed it, and God answered when they called. The Word of God and prayer must always go together (John 15:7; Acts 6:4), and so must prayer and obedience (Ps. 66:18).